W9-CBM-663

new garden design

daab

Cuando el hombre descubrió que podía controlar el desarrollo del mundo vegetal, el jardín se convirtió en un lugar donde descansar, jugar, reunirse en sociedad y disfrutar del placer de los sentidos. Desde el lejano "locus amoenus" de la civilización latina hasta los actuales jardines de inspiración zen, estos paraísos particulares son también un lugar perfecto para estar en contacto con la naturaleza, a la vez que para experimentar con el diseño y la arquitectura del paisaje. Los jardines que aquí se presentan ofrecen nuevas e interesantes interpretaciones de los tradicionales jardines de viviendas particulares, que, generalmente condicionados por la falta de espacio y por el contexto urbano que los rodea, brindan, al mismo tiempo, la posibilidad de encontrar soluciones novedosas y de experimentar con distintos materiales.

Depuis que l'homme a découvert qu'il pouvait diriger le développement du monde végétal, le jardin est devenu un lieu de détente, de plaisir, facilitant les relations sociales et permettant de profiter de tous ses sens. De ce lointain « locus amoenus » de la civilisation latine jusqu'aux jardins actuels d'inspiration zen, ces paradis particuliers sont autant de lieux parfaits pour établir des relations avec la nature, que pour découvrir le design et l'architecture du paysage. Les jardins présentés ici offrent des interprétations intéressantes et novatrices par rapport aux jardins traditionnels des maisons particulières généralement conditionnés par le manque d'espace ou par le contexte urbain qui les entoure. D'un autre côté, ces obstacles incitent à découvrir des solutions nouvelles et créatives et à tester différents matériaux.

Nel momento in cui l'uomo scoprì che poteva dirigere lo sviluppo del mondo vegetale, il giardino è diventato un luogo dove poter riposare, trascorrere piacevoli momenti di gioco e di svago, potenziare i rapporti sociali e godere del piacere sensoriale. Sin dal lontano locus amoenus della civiltà latina fino agli attuali giardini di ispirazione zen, questi angoli privati di paradiso sono anche un luogo ideale per stabilire rapporti con la natura, e al tempo stesso sperimentare con il disegno e l'architettura del paesaggio. I progetti presentati in questo libro offrono interessanti e nuove interpretazioni dei giardini tradizionali delle abitazioni private, che generalmente sono condizionati dalla mancanza di spazio o dal contesto urbano che li circonda. D'altronde, questi ostacoli servono da spunto per cercare di individuare soluzioni nuove ed immaginative e sperimentare con vari tipi di materiali.

Seitdem die Menschheit entdeckte, dass sie die Entwicklung der Pflanzenwelt lenken kann, wurde aus dem Garten ein Ort, an dem man Ruhe sucht, sich am Spiel erfreut, soziale Beziehungen pflegt oder sich den Sinnesfreuden hingibt. Seit der Zeit des „locus amoenus" der lateinischen Zivilisation bis zum heutigen Zengarten ist dieses ganz besondere Paradies auch der perfekte Ort, um die Natur zu erfahren und mit der Gartenarchitektur und Design zu experimentieren. Die Gärten, die wir Ihnen zeigen, sind neue und interessante Interpretationen der Gärten traditioneller Wohnhäuser, die im allgemeinen von zwei Faktoren geprägt sind: Platzmangel und die umgebende Stadtlandschaft. Gerade diese Hindernisse führen dazu, dass innovative und einfallsreiche Lösungen gefunden und neue Materialien eingeführt werden.

Ever since human beings discovered how to control the growth of plants, the garden has been a place in which they have found peace, enjoyed playing, cemented social relationships and revelled in sensory pleasure. From the faraway "locus amoenus" of Roman civilization to today's gardens inspired by Zen philosophy, these private paradises are ideal spots for communing with nature, as well as for experimenting with the design and architecture of landscape. The gardens presented here provide interesting new interpretation of the traditional garden attached to private houses, which are generally subject to spatial restrictions or the surrounding urban context. These obstacles, however, can stimulate both the discovery of both imaginative, new solutions and experiments with different types of materials.

.

Adèle Juhas-Barton, Landscaper + Toni Esteva, Architect | Majorca, Spain
Convent de la Missió Garden
Majorca, Spain | 2003

Adèle Juhas-Barton, Landscaper + Toni Esteva, Architect | Majorca, Spain
Garden in Majorca
Majorca, Spain | 2002

Alexander Oesterheld | Husum-Schessinghausen, Germany
Swimming Pond Garden
Neustadt, Germany | 2003

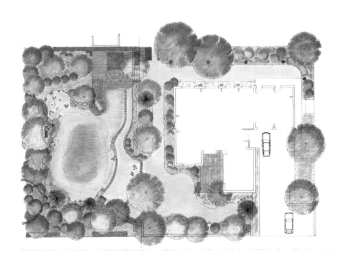

Ana Esteve Land | Barcelona, Spain
Garden in Sant Cugat
Barcelona, Spain | 2002

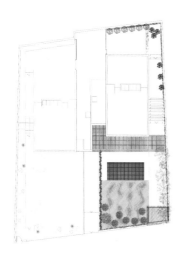

Bernhard Korte | Grevenbroich, Germany
Garden in Cologne
Cologne, Germany | 2004

Dangar Group | Double Bay, Australia
Balmain
Balmain, Australia | 2004

Dangar Group | Double Bay, Australia
Thomas St. Garden
St. Ives, Australia | 2004

Dry Design | Los Angeles, USA
McDonnell Garden
Santa Monica, USA | 2002

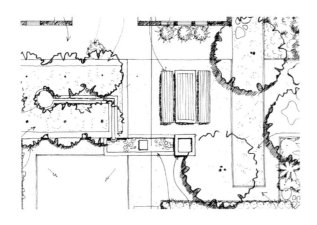

Enea Garden Design | Schmerikon, Switzerland
Garden in Zurich
Zurich, Switzerland | 2004

Faulkner & Chapman Landscape Design | Brighton, Australia
Residential Garden
Brighton, Australia | 2004

Feeny Mallindine Architects | London, UK
Notthinghill Garden
London, UK | 2004

Florence Lim, London | UK
Florence Lim Garden
London, UK | 2003

Fred-Jürgen Störner | Wesel, Germany
Bungalow
Wesel, Germany | 2004

GMP | Hamburg, Germany
Villa Alexandra
Riga, Latvia | 2003

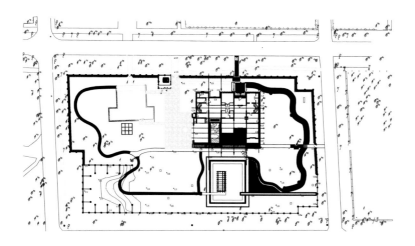

Ian Chee & Voon Wong | London, UK
Garden in London
London, UK | 2004

Juan Bautista Sirpo, Architect + Rosa Mª Ricci, Landscaper | Punta del Este, Uruguay
Stefani Garden
Punta del Este, Uruguay

Kaoru Sawada | Tokyo, Japan
Rise Garden
Tokyo, Japan | 2004

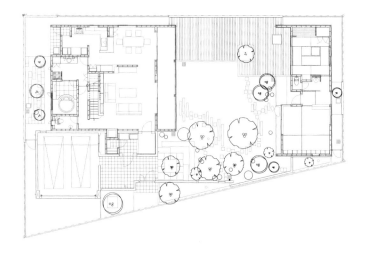

Laura Brucco Architect | Buenos Aires, Argentina
Laura Brucco Garden
Buenos Aires, Argentina | 2004

Marpa & Associates | Boulder, Colorado, USA
Mountains and Rivers
Boulder, Colorado, USA | 2002

McGregor + Partners | Sydney, Australia
Airia Apartments
Sydney, Australia | 2004

McGregor + Partners | Sydney, Australia
Atlas Apartment
Sydney, Australia | 2004

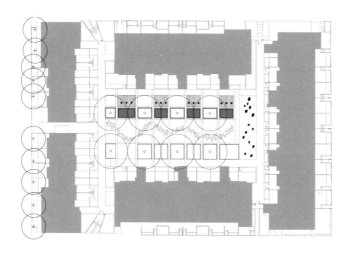

Munkenbeck + Marshall | London, UK
Garden in London
London, UK | 2004

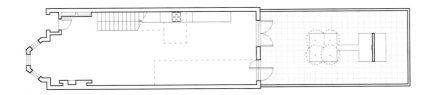

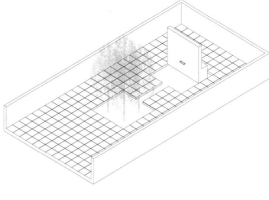

Out From the Blue + Mira Martinazzo, Designer | Melbourne, Australia
Maturucco
Surrey Hills, Melbourne, Australia | 2004

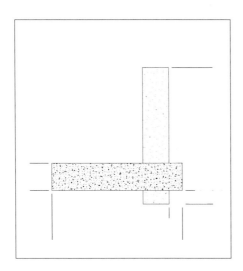

Out From the Blue | Melbourne, Australia
Biesse
Hawthorn, Melbourne, Australia | 2004

Out From the Blue + Loredana Ducco, Designer | Melbourne, Australia
Morris
Hawthorn, Melbourne, Australia | 2004

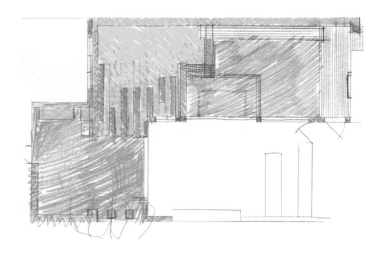

R. Thompson | Oxford, UK
R. Thompson Garden
Oxford, UK | 2004

Rush + Wright Associates | Melbourne, Australia
Douglas Street Garden
Melbourne, Australia | 2004

Rush + Wright Associates | Melbourne, Australia
Mt. Eliza
Melbourne, Australia | 2004

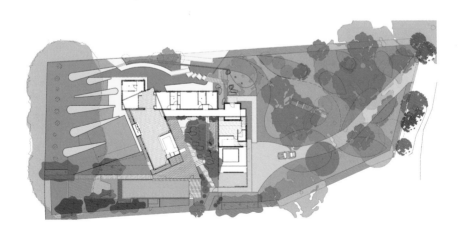

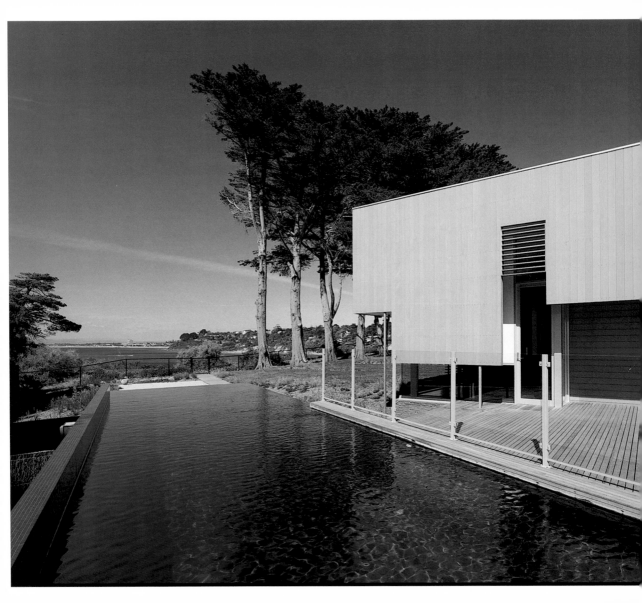

Satmoko Ball | London, UK
Hamersmith Grove Garden
London, UK | 2002

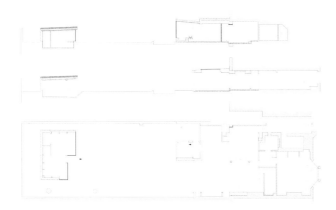

Satmoko Ball | London, UK
Hamersmith Grove Garden
London, UK | 2002

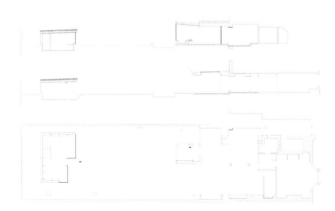

Schümmelfelder Stöcker Partner | Düsseldorf, Germany
Residential Garden
Cologne, Germany | 2004

Terence Conran
Conran Garden
London, UK | 2004

3:0 Landschaftsarchitektur + Robert Luger | Vienna, Austria
Flat-Roof Garden
Vienna, Austria | 2004

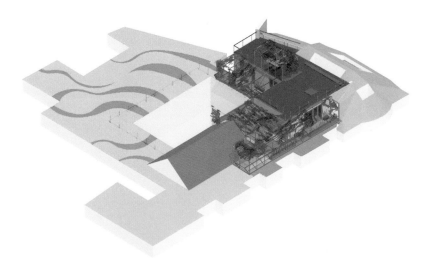

360° Landscape Architects | Surry Hills, Australia
Clovelly Garden
Sydney, Australia | 2003

360º Landscape Architects + Alex Popov + Janet Laurence | Surry Hills, Australia
Piper Point Garden
Sidney, Australia | 2004

Unknown
Garden Makeover
London, UK | 2004

Unknown
Quintas Garden
South of France | 2004

Adèle Juhas-Barton, Landscaper + Toni Esteva, Architect
Convent de la Missió Garden
Photos: © Pere Planells
Garden in Majorca
Photos: © Pere Planells

Alexander Oesterheld
In der Blankenau, 12, D-31632 Husum, Germany
P. +49 5027 294
www.die-gartenidee.de
Swimming Pond Garden
Photos: © Ferdinand Graf von Luckner

Ana Esteve Land
Freixa, 45, 08021 Barcelona, Spain
aesteve@land1988.com
Garden in Sant Cugat
Photos: © Jean Pierre Mongard / Ana Esteve

Bernhard Korte
Freier Landschaftsarchitekt, Frankenstrasse, 56, 41517
Grevenbroich, Germany
P. +41 2181 215454
Garden in Cologne
Photos: © Sabrina Rothe / Artur

Dangar Group
P.O. Box 438, Double Bay NSW 2028, Australia
P. +61 2 9369 3166
www.dangargroup.com
Balmain
Photos: © Murray Fredericks
Thomas St. Garden
Photos: © Murray Fredericks

Dry Design
5727 Venice Blvd., Los Angeles, CA 90019, USA
P. +1 323 954 9084
www.drydesign.com
McDonnell Garden
Photos: © Undine Pröhl

Enea Garden Design
St. Gallerstrasse, 36, 8716 Schmerikon, Switzerland
P. +41 55 286 2266
Garden in Zurich
Photos: © Sabrina Rother / Artur

Faulkner & Chapman Landscape Design
106 Cole St., Brighton 3186, Australia
P. +61 3 9596 0059
www.faulknerchapman.com.au
Residential Garden
Photos: © Shania Shegedyn

GMP
Elbchaussee, 139, Hamburg 22763, Germany
P. +49 40 88151-0
www.gmp-architekten.de
Villa Alexandra
Photos: © Guna Eglite

Feeny Mallindine Architects
P. +44 20 7405 7405
info@feenymallindine.com
Nottinghill Garden
Photos: © Peter Cook / View

Ian Chee & Voon Wong
Garden in London
Photos: © Henry Wilson / Red Cover

Florence Lim
Florence Lim Garden
Photos: © Henry Wilson / Red Cover

Juan Bautista Sirpo, Architect + Rosa Mª Ricci, Landscaper
Stefani Garden
Photos: © Ch.Sarramon / A. Cardinale

Fred-Jürgen Störmer
Am Spaltmannsfeld, 20, 46485 Wesel, Germany
P. +49 281 98680
Bungalow
Photos: © Sabrina Rothe / Artur

Kaoru Sawada
601, 2-27-8 Yoyogi Shibuya-ku, Tokyo 151-0053, Japan
P. +81 3 5350 2761
Rise Garden
Photos: © Satoshi Asakawa / Zoom

Laura Brucco Architect
Laura Brucco Garden
Photos: © Ch. Sarramon / A. Cardinale

Marpa & Associates / Landscape architects
Martin Mosko, principal
1275 Cherryvale Road, Boulder, Colorado, USA
P. +1 303 442 5220
www.marpa.com
Mountains and Rivers
Photos: © Alxe Noden

McGregor + Partners
21 C Whistler St., Manly, Sydney, Australia
P. +61 2 9977 3853
www.mcgregorpartners.com.au
Airia Apartments
Atlas Apartment
Photos: © McGregor + Partners

Munkenbeck + Marshall
135 Curtain Road, London EC2A 3BX, UK
P. +44 20 7739 3300
F. +44 20 7739 3390
mail@mandm.uk.com
Garden in London
Photos: © Dennis Gilbert / View

Out From the Blue
48 Church Street, Hawthorn, 3122, Australia
P. +61 3 9855 1950
www.outfromtheblue.com.au
Maturucco
Biesse
Morris
Photos: © Shania Shegedyn

R. Thompson
R. Thompson Garden
Photos: © Andrew Twort / Red Cover

Rush + Wright Associates
Level 11, 522 Flinders Lane, Melbourne 3000, Australia
P. +61 3 9649 7844
Douglas St. Garden
Photos: © Ben Wrigley
Mt. Eliza
Photos: © John Gollings

Satmoko Ball
21 D Bradbury Mews, Bradbury Street, London N16 8JW, UK
P. +44 207 254 5200
www.satmokoball.co.uk
Hamersmith Grove Garden
Photos: © Sue Barr / View

Schümmelfelder Stöcker Partner
Landschaftsarchitektur / Innerarchitektur
Ernst-Poensgen-Alle, 17, 40629 Düsseldorf, Germany
P. +49 211 304036
Residential Garden
Photos: © Sabrina Rothe / Artur

Terence Conran
www.conran.com01
Conran Garden
Photos: © Ken Hayden / Red Cover

3:0 Landschaftsarchitektur
NESTROYPLATZ 1/1, 1020 Vienna, Austria
P. +43 1 969 06 62
www.3zu0.com
Flat-Roof Garden
Photos: © Rupert Steiner

360° Landscape Architects
Level 5, 68-72 Wentworth Avenue, Surry Hills NSW 2010, Australia
P. +61 2 2921 2204
Piper Point Garden
Clovelly Garden
Photos: © Rodney Evans / All Angles

Unknown
Garden Makeover
Photos: © Jon Bouchier / Red Cover
Quintas Garden
Photos: © Guy Bouchet / Ana Cardinale

copyright © 2005 daab gmbh

published and distributed worldwide by
daab gmbh
friesenstr. 50
d - 50670 köln

p +49-221-94 10 740
f +49-221-94 10 741

mail@daab-online.de
www.daab-online.de

publisher ralf daab
rdaab@daab-online.de

art director feyyaz
mail@feyyaz.com

editorial project by loft publications
copyright © 2005 loft publications

editor Encarna Castillo
layout Ester Heredia
english translation Matthew Clark
french translation Jean Pierre Leyre
italian translation Maurizio Siliato
german translation Susanne Engler
copy editing Alessandro Orsi

printed in spain
Anman Gràfiques del Vallès, Spain
www.anman.com

isbn 3-937718-19-2
d.l.: B-14668-05

all rights reserved.
no part of this publication may be reproduced in any manner.